Still
HOME

Still

the essential poetry of SPARTANBURG

HOME

edited by
Rachel **Harkai**

HUB CITY writers project

2008

Edited by Rachel Harkai
Cover photograph by Justin Plakas
Cover and book design by Emily L. Smith

First printing, March 2008
Manufactured at McNaughton & Gunn, Inc., Saline, Michigan.

Library of Congress Cataloging-in-Publication Data

Still home : the essential poetry of Spartanburg / edited by Rachel
  Harkai.
     p. cm.
  ISBN 978-1-891885-59-4
  1. American poetry~South Carolina~Spartanburg County. 2.
  Spartanburg
County (S.C.)~Poetry. I. Harkai, Rachel, 1985- II. Hub City
Writers Project.
  PS558.S6S75 2008
  811'.6080975729~dc22
                              2007052529

Hub City Writers Project
Post Office Box 8421
Spartanburg, SC 29305
(864) 577-9349 • fax (864) 577-0188
www.hubcity.org

Contents

Introduction

I HAD ONLY BEEN IN SPARTANBURG FOR A WEEK OR TWO WHEN BETSY TETER, program director of the Hub City Writers Project, approached me about editing this anthology. With such an overwhelming number of talented poets living in the greater Spartanburg area, she told me it was about time that Hub City compiled a body of poems to define their efforts and to explore their connection to Spartanburg—a place so many working writers call home. I was immediately excited about the project—not only because of its genre, and by the opportunity to explore the unfamiliar territory of editing a collection, but by the prospect of familiarizing myself with my new home and its residents in a somewhat preternatural, literary way.

At the time, however, Spartanburg only seemed familiar to me in those discrete areas where its culture and history overlapped with stereotypes of Southern life. I knew that, like so many middling and somewhat sleepy areas of the American South, Spartanburg County was home to a Revolutionary War battlefield, a plantation or two left over from the Civil War era, and an unfortunate overabundance of abandoned mills that evidenced the death of the textile industry's Southern boom. With only these few preconceived notions of Spartanburg's cultural and historical identity, I wondered if I might lack the insight required to marry the individual works of these poets into an eloquent and unified intimation of the essential qualities of Southern life. My anxiety only heightened after sending out my preliminary batch of letters soliciting work. I was repeatedly told that, despite being thrilled about the project, most of these local poets did *not* feel that Spartanburg was finding its way into their writing.

This in mind, when I found myself nearing the end of all the reading, editing, compiling, and organizing that went into the formation of this collection, I felt somewhat similar, I imagine, to the therapist who succeeds in awakening his patient to some latent issue that has been permeating and affecting the patient's mental state since the earliest years of childhood. I had—right in front of me, on my very desk—seventy-five or so pages to prove that these poets had, in fact, been writing about life in Spartanburg all along.

The poets in this collection were raised in Spartanburg County, or are living here now, and their poems present its landscape in full panorama, stretching from Landrum's northern mountain views to the southernmost streets of rural Woodruff. In a recapitulation of, I believe, the French philosopher Deleuze, Jennie Neighbors writes in her poem "Thought": "Landscapes are a preparation for what will later appear as a set." How fitting then, that the natural beauty of the Carolina landscape and its components—rivers, pines, mountains, heat, even kudzu—is such a patent cohesive force among the poems here. Resembling the manner in which most themes of this collection are poetically tackled, the approach through which this landscape is explored is at once historical and neoteric. We are walloped with the plate tectonics of Fred Parrish's "Water Memory":

> What must it have been like to see
> these rivers turned aside?
> Cool channels deflected by hot rock.
> Moving water is a force in all three tenses
> where once all elemental hell broke loose.

Later, in Elizabeth Drewry's "Thanksgiving on Glassy Mountain," we are asked to reconcile this Creational explosion with the calmer natural world of the contemporary day:

We are far from the thin air of boardrooms,
spectacle of careers like kiting hawks on thermals:
the dihedral glide, the plummet.

We are left, then, somewhere in the middle, near John Lane's contemplative "Bethesda Road," groping to find where our current selves fit into such an extensive and elaborate past:

Years ago I wandered here as a boy
lonely among hardwoods, sifting nearby
creek gravel for bird points, pottery.
Now the moon tightens on this outcrop
of soapstone, stemmed where bowls
were chipped loose, fell clean of rock,
in another darkness, 5,000 years ago.

Through sometimes real and sometimes imagined visions of the past, this collection's exploration of the elements that define a place condenses the cycles of natural history from their grander scope within all of recorded time down to the everyday events of a single life. Here, these Spartanburg poets invite us into their kitchens, their yards, and sometimes, even into the homes of the unknowing next-door neighbor whose hanging blinds have been left ajar. Alex Richardson, among others, welcomes the reader to the sidewalks of Converse Heights—a neighborhood that flanks Spartanburg's downtown—in "Paradise Off Main":

We eat donuts and wrap ourselves in sheets
To topple into the hammock,
Wait for the paper-boy pedaling past,
Wobbling when he reaches for the news,
Then the postman in his wool shorts
And khaki-saucer hat.

With events both fantastic and mundane, the cycles of day-to-day life presented here involve everything from potty training, to parties, to landscaping the yard. Though they are often embedded inside of the sentimentality and reminiscence that inevitably envelop the concept of "home," these poets are not afraid to admit that family life is often anything but easy, as in Deno Trakas's "The Smaller House":

> My son flings his things and sonofabitches
> his sorryass father, downsized again.
> He hurls his own hard rock and wishes
> he could split this crib, this shitshack,
> this hell where death begins.

Of course, before too long, in any discussion regarding cycles of the natural world the inevitable will emerge: death. While reading the many books and chapbooks of writers I considered for this anthology, I was struck by a conspicuous preoccupation with dying that repeatedly surfaced. At first it seemed simply the product of common age. After all, a large number of writers whose work is here included are currently planted firmly in that strange space of middle age—a time when, I imagine, it is difficult not to feel bereaved, as one is forced to simultaneously watch children and parents grow old, while somehow retaining a feeling of remaining static. Yet, as I continued to screen more work from an increasingly large pool of poems, I began to find that Spartanburg's writers of all ages, ranging from recent college graduates to retirees, were writing about the deaths of loved ones, of strangers, and even about their own potential passing on. So often while reading these poems I found myself shuttled again into some Upstate cemetery, as in Mamie Morgan's "For Your Last Performance":

> Your death? Imagine a day ending at two in the
> afternoon. I numbered every night you didn't
> die as the sound of your air tank bumping
> against deck planks, spent all six cancer years
> watching from behind our rose bush that never
> bloomed. … The night I learned to drive I took
> my red Honda straight to Fernwood, slept
> on your grave, talked like I hadn't in years.

In the numbered list of bullet-points that comprise Philip Belcher's "Mid-Life," the poem's persona blankly admits his parents' submission to the inevitable passing of time: "My parents surrendered to age. They looked back at their childhoods, became pillars of salt." Young Woodruff native Emily Smith strikes a similar chord in "The House of My Mother is Falling Down":

> It's still melting and spoiling I worry about—
> strong Denver foundation crumbling like damp
> sugar, the body that made me funneling inward,
> amber silt in the center of the crowd.

Perhaps it is simply the plight of all writerly endeavors to be overwrought with the feeling of being in a vacuum—of remaining static while the surrounding world moves and changes. But perhaps not. More than one poet here experiments with raising the dead—with speaking to the ghosts of the South's complicated past. This past itself was, by leaps and bounds, the thematic aspect of this anthology I found most difficult to navigate.

"The house of dreams came to rest on the bottom shelf," writes Angela Kelly in "American Diaspora," embodying an attitude of regret that peeks through the surface of this collection on more than a few occasions. The verses of these poets recognize not only Spartanburg, but the South in general, as a space that is rife with traditions both good and bad. Many of these writers so far removed from my own young, Yankee psyche came of age during the Civil Rights movement, amidst segregation and its lingering ramifications. "I had black and white friends, but only white ones came over to play," Philip Belcher catalogues again in "Mid-Life." Butler Brewton reverts even further into Southern history in "Walnut Grove Plantation," a poem that shares its title with an old plantation in Spartanburg County:

> And there's this mournful singing
> Far beyond the tinkling glasses;
> There's a weeping people bending
> Cutting cane stalks for molasses;
> There're wagons on the hillside

Filled with hay for grazing cattle;
There're strong young men logging
Yet I hear their shackles rattle.

At first glance, I wondered whether poems such as these might simply be lingering too long within the aforementioned realm of regret. Now I am sure they do not. Poems such as this one embody a generation of contemporary Southern writers struggling to define itself and to explore its relationship to stigmas of Southern history. These poems invite change; they attempt to disentangle both poet and reader from the complications of the past, and they remind us, as Elizabeth Cox writes in "Say That":

The task, then, is to define that new piece,
to know its weight and structure, its edge
above the water, the new shoreline
that wobbles according to the water's lapping.

What I mean to say is that, while the moments embodied within any given poem may be static, the writers presented here are not. Though their work explores elements of the universal, these poets are crafting language in such a way as to invoke and inspire progress. They remind us that their community exists not within a single point in time, but on a continuum, refusing static notions of what defines the Southern literary landscape and demonstrating the role of the art of writing as a catalyst for change.

Rachel Harkai
Spartanburg, South Carolina

Rachel Harkai is the 2007–2008 Writer-in-Residence with the Hub City Writers Project. A native of Grand Rapids, Michigan, she is the recipient of bachelors degrees in Creative Writing and Comparative Literature from the University of Michigan. She has received Hopwood Awards for both poetry and nonfiction and is the former host of the Living Writers Show, a literary talk show on WCBN-FM 88.3 Ann Arbor. Her work has appeared in Michigan Quarterly Review, Spork, Portland Review, *and* Oleander Review. ⚜

Alex Richardson

Paradise Off Main

In the beginning, when it's all good,
We nurture ourselves with cigarettes and beer,
Take turns tip-toeing to the kitchen
Between our flights in the futon,
Then out stare the stars, our bodies a parabola,
Limbs interlocking like a cursive *l*
We eat donuts and wrap ourselves in sheets
To topple into the hammock,
Wait for the paper-boy pedaling past,
Wobbling when he reaches for the news,
Then the postman in his wool shorts
And khaki-saucer hat. These are the faces
To witness our proudest devotion,
Our sincerest vows,
Yes and *see you next weekend.*

Digging Up Azaleas Easter Eve

Wanda rigged a beaming flashlight, coal-miner style, to my hard hat.
I was the moon to every overworked worm in town,
A big dumb ass with one cartoon idea swaying
Between a shovel, a garden hose and Jose Cuervo.
Next door, Ms. Begonia served umbrella drinks,
Asked if I planned on digging all night,
Checking her wrist the way carpenters do at quitting time.
I assured her I was in it for the long haul,
Wouldn't rest till every azalea stump was heaped
On the curb as one muddy creature.
For three hours Wanda and Ms. Begonia chatted politics—
The state, the body, the orgasm—in whispers.
I loosened the maze of roots with each thrust,
Stabbing through sinews of burlap,
Piling up cool mounds of different-colored dirt
Till at once, I noticed them noticing me,
As if I'd sprouted from that same loam
Just to dig my own body back to hell.

Dancing Suite

I've moved a rocking chair into the bathroom
So when Penelope takes five from her dance recital,
I'll have someplace to sit. She twists her body on the pot
Like a quarter ride at the grocery, then clutches the sides smiling.
Sit there daddy. Close door daddy.

I flip the Cosmo ads, older beauties, lanky-necked as giraffes,
Till she hands me Kermit's book
On the proper procedures and techniques for successful, stress-free
evacuation.
The key, Kermit says, is to understand it's a process.
Just relax, I say, it'll come.

I sit in my corner like a dog
Who's learned to beg from a distance;
My eyebrows rise when I hear the deliberate sprinkle,
The emphatic plop. She dips her head between her knees,
Look daddy, it just come out my body.

I hold her hand through the rest: wiping, flushing.
It's the coda of swirling water
That sends her chirping through the house,
I'm the nakey jaybird.

The Geometry of Commitment

By the time the clock's big hand had nearly circled
The small hand, the therapist had given us the goods;
Marriage is not a 50/50 proposition;
The best you can hope for is 100% half the time.
My brow furrowed like an obedient spaniel's.
He whistled on, *meaning you get what you want*
Half the time; the other half you don't.

I should've known better,
But I felt after an hour I could try:
Yes, I blabbed, it's like parallel play;
You each do your own thing,
Sharing blocks to build separate mazes.

His smile sent me to kindergarten,
As he removed his horned-rims and squeezed
Wanda's knee. *No, there are no straight lines,*
Not in nature or in marriage, no straight lines
Anywhere. On the wall, the big hand
Began a victory lap while I leaned back,
Stretching my legs on the square rug.

Philip Belcher

A Man Over Forty Discover His Right Brain
  and Falls in Love with Her

And this is not an entirely happy
occurrence. It's as if he's discovered
a sister he's never known.
It's not that she's homely, or slow,
but rather so unfamiliar that identical
parentage seems unlikely. Her hair
is walnut brown, like his, but with a swath
as red as apples falling down one side.
Uncut, unbrushed, it hangs wherever
it will around her olive face, a face
that looks nothing like the pasty mask
he's grown under office lights.
Her jeans are loose but show legs
and thighs tight from use.
Oh, and they seem to speak different
languages, or maybe just very different
dialects of English. They communicate
better through motions. He points and names,
points and names. She sweeps her hands
through the air like branches and makes sounds
like the wind. If she weren't his sister,
he might find her attractive, as opposites
are said to do, and take her as a mistress,
leaving her early in bed to write poems
about how mismatched they are.

Then he would take her to see their parents,
who would be surprised that these children
had met after all these years and fallen in love.
They would warn him in private of her tendency
to break rules and to slow the natural progression
toward wealth and the assumption of middle class
values, not to mention the perils of incest.
As usual, his parents would be partly right.
At his age, he should be beyond infatuation
with her strangeness. He will wonder
over time whether they are compatible.
He will wish they'd met as children,
that they'd grown together as siblings,
comfortable enough to drop by
without warning, knowing each other
well enough to finish the other's sentences.

Estate Planning

My wife bought an urn to hold my ashes
just as a precaution and set it on the table
in the sunroom. Two brass handles protrude
like ears. Bands of pale enamel alternate
with stone the color of dust, the lid a small pagoda
topped with a marble nut.

She moves it around from time to time
to see where she'll like me most.
Different rooms, different heights.
Eye-level and out of children's reach,
but not too high to clean with the feather
duster she used once to stroke my dimpled hip.

The state requires a permit to float
your bones along the coast or spray
what's left into Appalachian air,
so she'll keep me close on the mantel
beside the clock to settle
and preside over life in the den.

Mid-Life

After Lisel Mueller

1. I was born in the South in an in-between time.

2. My country sent a spy to fly over its enemy, and the enemy shot it down. For thirty more years we scoured the sky for mushroom clouds.

3. I had black and white friends, but only white ones came over to play.

4. Three assassinations, two white one black, were followed by a shot to the moon.

5. No line divided family and church. A black and white fence divided the country.

6. Mother and father, brother, two sisters: we learned distance early. Over time, we moved away.

7. Saturday nights, we lined up our Sunday shoes for inspection. Little soldiers lacking polish.

8. Sunday afternoons, the hot drone of single engine planes while I napped in the grassy cup of a choked well.

9. Two decades of school and books and I a sieve instead of a sponge.

10. Living to work, not working to live. I do not remember my son's second year.

11. Years of living in the future, paying attention only to the calendar. The calendar was a list of things to do.

12. Screens and emails replaced phone calls and letters. I was protected from intimacy by machines.

13. My in-laws decided that 39 years together was enough. My wife learned to fear desertion.

14. No poems flowered for twenty years. Even now the buds hug themselves tightly.

15. Planes destroyed towers. Our pride dragged itself under the shrubbery to sulk.

16. My parents surrendered to age. They looked back at their childhoods, became pillars of salt.

17. The piano in Barnwell is silent. Disease has turned my father's fingers into castanets.

18. Parent to parent and child. I live in an in-between time.

Variations on the Word Chain

After Margaret Atwood

This is not a pretty word,
a word you would repeat
as a mantra or tape
to your mirror to greet you
in the morning, that is
unless you think of the daisy chain
you made when you were a child
by linking the green ends
of dead daisies in little loops,
but even that has a vaguely
unsavory sexual connotation
of bodies hooked together
in the eighties. There is also
the gold watch chain that hung
from my grandfather's side
vest pocket. But, for the most part,
the first thought is one of restraint,
the chain link fence that kept
you and your puppy in and out
of danger. And this one use
prompts a chain reaction
of firing synapses as one thought
hooks to another, the chain gang
walking in their abbreviated steps
and striped shirts picking up

trash on Highway 9, the chain
of custody required by the law
for the evidence that put them there,
the chain of command of the officers
who arrested them or of soldiers,
among whom the chain is so long
that it spans the Atlantic, connecting
armchair warriors here with just shaving
boys in Iraq whose fondest thought
is to roll a cart by their mother's
stockinged leg down the aisle
of the grocery chain or to sit
with Jennifer near the back
of the theatre bearing the name
of a chain like *Consolidated*
or *Regal*, corporate names
not slowing their interest
in undoing zippers and buttons
and other chains that might
hook clothes together in the dark,
to spend a few days composing
a chain letter to collect
unusual stamps and exotic
signatures from strangers
unfettered by personal knowledge
of the originator, to see
the veiled blue mountains
linked in their North-South chain
that somehow feel like home.

Natural History

An inch of skin from my thumb hung
from the metal edge of the boat seat
like a thin strip of bacon,

half the width of a Band-Aid, if that.
The remnant trough was raw for a day,
covered with ointment, milky slick.

For days skin from the sides slumped
into the wound, rolled in like waves, folded
over and in to leave a pale pink trail.

Trauma only speeds what happens anyway.
We slough our skin in sheets each day,
never completely new, not enough left to see

the difference between who we are and who we were.
I envy the black snake I saw scraping
himself new against the warm brick wall.

He left a whole sleeve behind,
turned and considered who he used to be
with his divining tongue

before slipping away.
I want to open my own museum of skin,
where I can visit and learn for once who I have been.

Fred Parrish

Spring

That wind through the trees this afternoon
sang to me all a long sweet time, rounded off
my hard edges and not to be attained angle of repose.
Impossible dome of cobalt verging on prussian above
the scream of the miter saw, meristematic promise of
green
pulsing everywhere mostly beyond eye's reach; haven
for a sweep of warblers heading North.
This time of year there's a world above our heads,
coupled lives unfolding their ten thousand year song
and dance,
stage left, stage right and boy they pull it off
each time without a standing ovation.
We should be breathless; for one more chance
to be standing there as the curtain rises on Spring.

Water Memory

There are streams gone deep into the
slate belt, cutting ribbed patterns east
and south in what was once volcano land,
drainage basins vying for the rain's attention.
God must have held a dicot leaf sunward
to show the audience in Eden
how a divide breaks water into parts.
Down old Carolina run Neuse, Tar, Uwharrie.
What must it have been like to see
these rivers turned aside?
Cool channels deflected by hot rock.
Moving water is a force in all three tenses
where once all elemental hell broke loose.
Can you imagine the impact zone feel
to this place when the heat began to leave?
Haw, Cape Fear, Catawba, they talk to us now,
Running toward salt, remembering fire.

P.L. Thomas

billboard

(You! *Driver*) "Come to MARLBORO COUNTRY":
a cowboy's face looming over passing
cars with passengers racing, just lighting
like the cowboy's massive fist; flat, paltry,
and weather-beaten, the billboard stands tall
and proud—a god-head begging for money,
promising a land of milk and honey.
He pushes both regular and menthol.

MARLBORO COUNTRY: *Do come*. Cough and gag
in the blackened swirling smoke, walk on low,
lifeless plains where tobacco once would grow
and light your decorated cancer fag.
Go ahead! Read the big words and inhale
the clear, clean manhood—the photographed smell.

drawn to two

I

Speed

Here I am fifty—
        half a life
ago tearing rumbling charging along
mountain roads   up and down the Saluda grade
driven by speed   the leaning and revving

on two wheels
        Harley-Davidson. Then
young reckless careless   except for speed.

But those were days
of Marlboros and Budweiser
            leathers   no helmet
before children   only the wife's fears   like

a fallen phone-line
        the pole I have to climb
the wires I have to restore
          fusing anonymous
conversations   calls for help   emergencies
tying people back together
        as I break away

the seat holding only one   only me

alone.

II

Running

               The years peeled away
the wind stripping me down to father
                     no leathers
smokeless   all the lines connected
              dial tones

replacing two wheels with shoes for jogging
the breeze gentle as my wife's contentment
bliss at her
       healthy husband grounded
breathing hard against the loop of my own
design pointless laps
          the throttle rumbling
inside my chest
       moved up from between my legs
the desire of my thighs
        jailed by heaving ribs

nylon rubber   the thumping of strides
I imagine myself chrome polished   black

red wings   Harley-Davidson
        two wheels
long distance direct.

III

Pedaling

As if I were falling backward   a man
in my forties keeping conversations intact
from behind a desk
            the pole no longer

between my heels my knees my thighs
replaced by a boy's toy
                bicycle two wheels
driven by my legs
            now pistons direct

to a chain drive crawling the same mountain
of my youth   the grade reborn under me
pedaling   my wife a woman I didn't marry

suffering through a cracked rib
                    broken collar
bone from leaning too far too slow
the recklessness gone
                gray bearded   collect

I pedal nearly unconscious ears ringing like
a call I must answer   emergency   two wheeled
and charging calling me red wings.

IV
Motor

                    Yes fifty
buying another two wheels   Harley-Davidson
resurrected Phoenix rumbling between
my thighs hog wallowing in the rumbling
no longer speed but sensation
the seat built for two
                    my wife
behind me liberated dialed in to the cycles
of the motor built for feel
                    vibrating us
together husband wife red-winged
charging recklessly leaning
against each other shaking us conscious
awake waking to the telephone poles
passing us marking our loops up
through down the mountains there
regardless of us or the wheels
following asphalt   us

          drawn to two wheels

Marcel Gauthier

Peaches and Firecrackers

Dropping down from
one Carolina to the other, we witness
like garish casinos in a deserted landscape
the signs. At first it's strange,
the two together, the gargantuan font,
but a dogged redundancy
seals the courtship: a flame-
colored peach exploding
in the mouth, th' exploding
firecracker surprising
as a peach—a metonymy of pleasure
in every bite or bang.

As if God has settled
on a perpetual Eden
laced with highways
and planted at every exit
forbidden fruit, temptation
in between, so when we stop
to refuel, as we inevitably
must, no matter how
pious we started at the border,
we blurt *what the hell*
and pay and drive away
loaded and giddy and ripe
with knowledge.

Kudzu

What I'd heard about
this alien, this nihilist,
this barbarian and conqueror
hadn't adequately indoctrinated me
not to see
beauty
in its abstract geography, its
lake-like shimmer
in the sun and breeze,
its merely whispering what lay beneath
of stone and shrub and tree.

Faced with the fact
that life as we know it
will end unless we act,
then asked to choose—until
a poet painted for me
something more wondrous out of
what once lived and what might be, I'd choose,
I think, like others before, exactly
what I see
and drown incredulous.

Scott Neely

Balsam. Wet Pine

Balsam. Wet pine
smell, walking
the mountain's back.

The old growth
heart of God
draws down clouds
and shrouds itself:

the piney spine
and pitch of the ridge
in fog.

Dusk comes
with bats
in the valley below us,
hunting over the river
that cut this hill
steep and round
and soaks its roots
in the heart of God.

Edwin C. Epps

Mr. Sandburg's Place

The poet's
path through the pines
wound up
and round
and into the cleanest imagined space
on his property.
We huffed and noted sweet gum
and pitcher plants,
a snake,
even a crazed jogger careening
down from the top.
On we trudged,
losing a few
to tobacco and heaviness along the way,
our stubbornness the emblem of our kinship
with the seer and his vision.

At last the granite outcrop flared before us;
we stumbled over roots and mud
and our own hesitation
and occupied each our own spot:
a Park Service bench
or plot of cold hard stone,
backs against the trees,
eyes raised in contemplation,

and then we wrote.

On Hearing of the Death in His Sleep
of John Lee Hooker, 21 June 2001

John Lee Hooker dead
new thunder from the heavens
yeah boom boom boom boom

After Reading James Still

When last my father traveled up
into the hills,
he knew that he was dying.
Unspoken, that knowledge informed us all
and circumscribed our movements up and down.

At night he labored in his bed
to wrest insufficient grudging air
from greedy, too thin breezes,
and managed
and, though he never said it,
was thankful for the time.

Out hiking one day,
I was instantly startled
by the shucked skin of a copperhead
and reminded of the reason we had come.

Thomas Johnson

Note on a Nightscape after the Style of Hiroshige

As a broken pen spills ink on paper

at a cost of words never to be spelled

or heard, so the beams of this brief moon

I'd hoped to read your eyes by only splashed

and scattered for an instant on the surface

of the lake, not yielding light enough

to see the slightest feature of your face.

And so the writing of a poem which was meant

for you alone must now await the perfect

conjugation of another time and moon and place.

Nine Haiku for the Poet Basho from One of His Students:

Farewell Verses

i.
Pack these words, sir: they
would follow you like songbirds
over the long march.

ii.
In the doorway skulks
a dog with pleading eyes: "Take
me. Take me with you."

iii.
The plum tree's dying
in the garden; if you stayed,
she would come back too.

iv.
The bird had mastered
how to chirp "Hello"; now he's
got to crow "Farewell."

v.
Each poet's eye scans
the same sky differently,
but for long goodbyes.

vi.

Shadow on the pool!
A black cat waits a final
word from one gold fish.

vii.

Take the caged goldfinch
with you. Teach him what we need
to know. Send him back.

viii.

These walls are paper
thin, but they will hold the ink
of one last poem.

ix.

Over the entrance
to the temple, written in
blood, one word: "Poet!"

Frances Hardy

Storage

Mama used to journey to the backyard garden
in the hot sun
toiling and pulling out the weeds.
She ventured each day from the shed to the dirt
to rake in her harvest
to bring forth
blood red tomatoes
long, crisp string beans
yellow squash trying to curve themselves into the earth.

Stopping under the shade of trees
denying herself rest
to pluck and pull plums
to lean into muscadines
getting ready
for Joseph's famine—
foreseeing
knowing
sharing
shouting
as she marched up and down the rows,
"Prepare, children, prepare
for the day when there will be no Benjamins.
While you can, children,
Put away for hard times

Put away for your brothers and sisters
who have no storehouse.
Be Joseph."

John Lane

Sweet Tea

God rested on the seventh day, but early in the morning,
    before the sun strained into the Southern sky,
    she made sweet tea from scratch. She boiled the water
    in a black kettle, put in the orange pekoe bags
    and let them stand as the water perked, and then
    she did what gods know to do: She heaped in Dixie
    Crystal sugar while the brew was still warm as the day.

For God so loved the world she made sweet tea. For she served
    the tea to anyone who admired for creation. To anyone
    walking down the street of the wet new neighborhood,
    to the mailman delivering early on that next day
    of that second week, to the milkman in his truck, the black
    man working in the yard, to the white man selling peaches
    door-to-door. On God's sidewalk there was an X scratched
    by hobos. They knew to come to God's back door and you'd
    get a plate of leftovers and all the sweet tea you could
    drink. They knew the sugared pints of contentment. They drank
    sweet tea from God's back steps and went on their wandering
    way again.

For God knows sweet tea fills with love and refreshment from
    any long train. For sweet tea is safe as an oak forest
    camp. Sweet tea, clinks in jelly jars. Sweet tea,
    sweeter as it stands. For God's sake we brew it

like a religion. For God's sake we carry it now in styrofoam
cups in cars. We drink it in winter. We drink it always.

And this poem would not lessen sweet tea's place in the creation.
Sweet tea is not fading from the Southern towns
like the Confederate flag. It lives in houses all over town.
Black folk brew it as often as white folk. Take the flag off
the state capitol. It doesn't mean anything to me.
But leave be my sweet tea, a recipe for being civil.

This poem stands cold sweet tea up as God's chosen beverage.
The manifest Southern brew. When sad I draw figures
in the condensation of glasses of sweet tea. I connect
the grape leaves on the jelly jar, cast out any restaurant
that will not make it from scratch. When lonely I go
to the house of my beloved.

For I love a woman who makes sweet tea late at night to eat with
Chinese Food. For her hands move like God's through the ritual.
For it is as if she had learned it along with speaking in
tongues. For I love the way her hands unwrap the tea bags
and drop them in the water. For I love the unmeasured sugar
straight from the bag, the tap water from deep in the earth.
For these processes are as basic for love as making love.
For our bodies both are brown like suntans inside from years
of tea. For sweet tea is the Southern land we share, the town,
the past. When we kiss it is sweet tea that we taste as
our lips brush. When we are hot it is sweet tea we crave.
When we have children it will be sweet tea.
And they will learn tea along with Bible stories and baseball.

Nostalgia for Work and Deep Mountains

Along the broad valleys peasants extend a history
of potatoes and wheat. Each steady worker, evening
folding behind him, pushes barrows like boats
over rutted trails to home, smoke spiraling, like messages
rising off the river of dawn, the blue haze
in the distance, the woods on the mountainside.

A short man slowly scratches his curving side,
as if the spot held affection for him, a history
of skin and hand, white rigid meeting slab of blue
nail; this is the final hour before another evening
unfolds its comfort and soup speaks its quiet message,
the bowls waiting on the table, spoons deep as frigates.

He climbed the rigging once, not long schooners
but tall ships, and his size kept him to the side
of the mast, where the ropes bowed and the messages
were hung with signal flags. He remembers no history
as he walks into the yard on this normal evening,
no special date to mourn often as the hills turn blue.

He notices his wife has set the evening table, blue
bottoms of the soup bowls, that deep curve of dories
bobbing on a calm sea shocks him free of the evening,
and the frightening fall, plunging over the side

into the sea; he is a farmer now with no history
to sidle into—soup only—domestic messages.

His wife sends her clear love through the messages
of soup and table; if the spoon is clean, it is blue,
and this event she chronicles in the long history
of this valley; she knows not his memories of sloops,
or even the tiny scar scripting his burly right side
though her hands stay steady on his back late evening.

Bethesda Road

Years ago I wandered here as a boy,
lonely among hardwoods, sifting nearby
creek gravel for bird points, pottery.
Now the moon tightens on this outcrop
of soapstone, stemmed where bowls
were chipped loose, fell clean of rock,
in another darkness, 5,000 years ago.
I click on my flashlight, the stone
clutter is everywhere.
Wildflowers push through broken bowls
at my feet—Queen Anne's lace,
here at the edge of the fields,
chicory, tight buds in the night—
like the worked stone itself flowers.
Below, in the remaining hardwood groves
shadows sink in the trunks of oaks.

A possum prowls thick rows
of pines near the range of the next hill.
Then, stopped in my flashlight beam
it haunches up in a small country of trees.
I click off the light and the possum
given night back like a room to enter,
scuttles through the pines.
I follow into its darkness.

For miles I hear the song
of its feet through dry pine,
cut-over fields, a last still stream,
into the first tentative lights of houses.
And finally I stand at the edge of yards
and listen as the possum rifles cans—
this night and all it accommodates
its only vision, and mine,
as the world around us sleeps.

My Dead Father Watches Traffic Pass

I hadn't asked my dead father for advice,
but he uses this chance to tell me again
about saving money, extra work, and how not
to end up broke: "Never buy anything on credit.
When you get a dollar, shave a little piece of it
off for the bank," he says, watching cars pass.

It's not how I'd spend a summer Sunday evening,
but my dead father has backed my truck off
the main drag, and we're watching traffic pass.
He's planning my whole week: Friday night, up on Main
watching the country people come to town;
Saturday, the same with "the coloreds."
My dead father's idea of entertainment
is cheap, but it only ends when the week does.
"Don't you want to do anything else?" I ask.
"It's Sunday," he says, and he's intent to sit right here.

I tell him we don't do that now, country people
go to Wal-Mart, even on Sunday, and you can get shot
for looking at someone the wrong way, any day
of the week, and downtown is nothing but pawn shops,
wig shops, and jewelry stores anyway.

"I see what you mean," he says. "Looks like more cars
Now then people. Ever think about opening a filling station?"
He asks. I'm employed, I explain one more time. I've
got summers off is all. "Good money and changing oil,
especially summers. Still have your evenings free."

My Dead Father Visits My Mother

I knew he would ask, but it took my dead father
a week. "She's across town," I say. "We should drive
over there and see her." He looks at his hands
and shuffles his feet like a boy of fourteen.
"Oh come on, we won't stay long. And don't worry.
She can't see you," I say. "You're dead."

In the car I tell my father about my mother,
how she's never married again, how we had a scare
this year, a small stroke. "She's slowing down,"
I say. "She's over 70." He pulls out his old
wallet and looks at his last picture of her,
my mother, still in her thirties, her hair black
as my dead father's mood. "Cheer up," I say.
"You can sit here in the car if you want."

"This is it," I say, and pull up the safety brake.
I can see my mother's reading lamp on in the den.
"The house is paid for," I say. "And she had a car
'till last year." My dead father is walking slower
than usual as I open the front door with my key.
"Mama, we're home!" He slips his elbow in my ribs,
and I'm smiling at how he's quieted down.
"Who is with you?" she says, creeping in
from the den. "Just us chickens," he says.

Deno Trakas

After Reading Your Dead Father Poems

for JL

I ask if I can meet your dead father.
You hesitate, say Nobody sees him but me,
but then, of course, you invite me over.

When I pull up to your house on McDowell Street,
you're sitting on the porch,
holding a glass of strawberry tea.

How does this work? I ask.
He's right there, you say, pointing to the rocker.
Pleased to meet you, Mr. Lane.

He wants to know if you want a beer.
No thanks, tea will be fine,
and you go inside, leaving me with your dead father.

I try to imagine him sitting there but I've only seen one photo,
from the war, before he married your mama—he was younger
than we are now—we're the age he died

(of heart trouble, you used to say, before you could say suicide)
and I imagine him one of us, a high school friend who's been away
and wants to know what ever happened to what's-her-name.

I want to ask What brings you to the neighborhood?
or Have you seen my father? and How's he doing?
But I feel like a fool now that I'm here.

John's told me a lot about you, I say. He and I are buddies,
we both like cheeseburgers with slaw, basketball, tennis,
poetry—we're both democrats—I imagine him smiling as I ramble—

and both of us have lost our fathers, though mine's been gone
only two years and, well, you've come back.
I'm jealous, I say, I miss my father.

You return, hand me my tea. Y'all having a nice chat?
Yeah, but a bit one-sided, I'd say. I told him I'm jealous,
you have your father back.

He's a pain in the ass, always after me to change my oil
or throw out store-bought eggs, always smoking those damn Camels.
But he has a knack for ratchets, I'll give him that.

How did you come back, and why? I finally ask.
Yeah, you say, that's a good question.
I watch you listen and await your translation:

He says there's things I need to know, especially now I'm his age
and I don't have a son—a man needs a son—
he wanted to tell me that.

You've got it backward, you say to him,
a son needs a father.
And even I can hear his answer: Here I am.

The Smaller House

*All that happens when I get something
wonderful like this award is that my
neuroses move into a larger house.*
—Ahkil Sharma

We've moved into a smaller house,
mother, father, daughter, son and dog,
far from convenience but close
to claustrophobia, a "fixer upper,"
a fixated dump whose sewer line clogs.

In the masterless bedroom, too small
for a king, my wife hammers
nails like migraines into the wall,
then hangs our children on books,
and when the phone screams, shivers.

Her mother wants to see our little nook,
she'll bring a plant, she'll help us clean
and Martha Stewart our squalor—she'll even cook.
My daughter, convicted to unpacking dishes,
squashes roaches to Rage Against the Machine.

My son flings his things and sonofabitches
his sorryass father, downsized again.
He hurls his own hard rock and wishes
he could split this crib, this shitshack,
this hell where death begins.

On my belly I slither the pitchblack
crawlspace to find the furnace and light the pilot—

insects skitter and spiderwebs claw my back—
but I'm desperate for one small success
below these joists of dry rot.

I bump and fumble and finally gain access
to the inner switches, light a match—
the saving flame catches, the furnace groans
like a testy god. Outside the dog scratches
the patch of grass, trying to find a bone.

Defining Family

For CBW

After every conceivable
effort, test and cost
and prayer, magical
science fails.

Her doctor calls—
he's sorry—he explains.
Outside the snow falls,
muffling the expected news.

Never, then. So.
She tucks herself in
the recliner, an angle of no
repose, tries to read

the blurry words,
The Handmaid's Tale—
how ironic, how absurd—
she'll tell her husband,

an occupied man
who works in the wing
to fill the span
of winter and then deliver spring.

It won't be enough—
the loss, like wind,
will howl against the luff
of their home.

Beyond the panes of the window
other people's children
frolic and plop in the snow,
wave their arms to be angels.

Labor Day, Pen and Spade

For SH

I dig too, hand and arm,
but in a smaller, private yard.
Last summer's droughted grass
has come back weedy lush.

An expert once explained to me
there's no such thing as a weed,
only a plant in the wrong place,
and here there should be grass.

So I yank up plants misplaced.
Usually I manage to clear the surface,
sometimes I even get roots
and depth, usually not.

I'd like to think I have a skill,
my fingers managing the soil,
weeding, planting, spreading lime
and fertilizer with precise timing,

but mine is a fallible instinct
and no one who's expert thinks
my meager work is worth advice,
so I'm left to learn my own devices.

My judgment is unsettled—
some of the weeds are pretty
with clusters of purple flowers,
and I'd like to make allowance.

But I go with what I see around,
trim, level, uniform lawns—
I pull the weeds efficiently,
the purple flowers snap off easily.

Mamie Morgan

Watering the Plants with Milk

She doesn't remember how to say things: the green leaves
of that magnolia tree are, after all, only green.

May's neurotic promises, the cactus he brought
home surviving in heat that comes, as always, too soon.

The custodial work of the yard, a light
left on somewhere in the house when it needn't be.

It's like this, she thinks: that first piece of moon come out midday,
some slice of veil. Worse, spotting that piece from the insides of a car.

A moon in *pieces*, for Christ's sake,
the sun out alongside it—this weightless betrayal after all of the years.

She's gone flat in his rusted lawn chair, her sweaty thigh-backs
accepting the rigid pattern of iron grid.

He sculpts. Whittles bowls from rhododendron root.
Weaves old pantyhose onto a loom—somehow it comes up carpet.

He is wary: her vacant stare from the back porch, all the blank lined pages
browning in the grass. Some cheap comparison to money tossed into flame.

She remembers her old apartment's pale green walls, the sudden
specificity of color rushing like a word—*verde verde verde*.

Or, the navy hooded sweatshirt doused in woodsmoke she lost years ago at camp.
That collapse of autumn—she wonders if it's possible to shove all that back
    inside of her.

Before they were lovers, he begged her to come
write on his back porch, *I'd love to paint*

the way you tug at that bottom lip with your teeth.
After, only: *I like the way you make me feel.*

Here's the thing: she'd sell a poem for a compliment
to anyone who might take it, if only for a while,

to even his dog she's pretending to like,
petting just the length of his nose, and with only her forefinger.

She wants to tell him a story about her childhood,
about an experiment that won her third place in the science fair.

She'd sprinkled marigold seeds into three pots
and spent the month watering one with water,

one with milk, and the last with nothing at all.
She'd thought of her mother breast feeding, felt sure

the milk would make the marigold. But only one week later:
rotten dirt, molded leaves. None of it making sense.

There is the living, but also the living. She wants to tell him
a story that says: you make me miss every city in the world.

Instead, he sketches her naked and facedown, not to sell,
wraps her in glassine paper, hides her behind the washing machine

against Juan Logans, the stolen Claude Howell, and others.
He thinks, it's not that she's stopped listening.

He comes on top of her, saying *the one*, and she's remembering a portrait
he'll never paint of her: that day, as a small girl, she cleaned the gutters

of her family's mountain home with bare hands, caring little
about the mudded shirt sleeves of her turtleneck

or that the five dollars promised her would be paid
out of pocket by some grandmother she hated.

The satisfaction, though, of filthy leaves against her face.
She's stopped listening. She wants for him to grow a beard

or take up doing nothing at all. It does not occur to her
to look at his naked body and find it foreign.

Is it too easy to say the needle stuck on a record?
Well then, the needle stuck on a record.

To undergo a dock in springtime: the simple blonde two by fours
lined against black water (knee deep, only, or bottomless).

For the waters to still be cold and to feel that cold. But she merely holds
onto the maintenance of a bought yard in May—the benign cut grass, the mutt.

I will see you in the morning, she says, when she finally says
what she needn't. *I will see you in the morning. I will see you in the morning.*

from *For Your Last Performance*

Rosewood Lane, 1993

Smashing china against walls settled into the gentle removal of doors from their hinges. During August's last rain, the stacked heel of your emerald espadrille frayed like a hammock stretched too tight between trees. If memory is a game, those were the big bucks. The way you smoked like a boy and laughed like a man is a nickel tripping down steps. Your death? Imagine a day ending at two in the afternoon. I numbered every night you didn't die as the sound of your air tank bumping against deck planks, spent all six cancer years watching from behind our rose bush that never bloomed. Our double-humped front yard opened under fists like a trundle. My mother left you to mother me while she dried on our street-side, us kids took days digging a swimming pool with bare hands. Molly and I grated the dirt with our fingernails while your sons tapped hollow beats with the dead side of a shovel. What I mean to say: what is more spent than dried tears? Sometimes now I forget when was was or when when was and fit you false inside our Maine summer stories: I could have sworn the days were smack with children holding sparklers double-fisted, you poking holes inside our firefly jars. Is it too late for truth-telling? Most nights I wanted you to stop fighting, hurry up and die already, stop requiring that we watch. The night I learned to drive I took my red Honda straight to Fernwood, slept on your grave, talked like I hadn't in years.

Fall Term, 2005

Vomit in the house,
a red solo cup tossed
in the yard.

—haiku assignment, Martin Eichart, college sophomore

I am telling the class to stop writing
about being wasted, that being wasted

is fine, but that the lack of specificity
troubles me. Troublesome as a broken cork

in a bottle of Sangiovese at the start
of a very bad first date, when I wouldn't wish sobriety

upon them or anyone. Really, I am talking to Martin
who is tapping an empty water bottle against his desk.

I am talking to Martin
but saying *class* the way we disguise ourselves

as who we partially are. Listen, as a little girl
I thought New Orleans was an island and that to go there

you were expected to behave and wear stockings.
My grandmother, Polly, seemed to fern her way

across the Pontchartrain in a sage green dress,
the queen of parishes and the perished.

We sat in restaurants alongside women in peacock-feathered hats.
We visited Aunt Gladys while she styled the manes

of poodles and Cuban ladies who delivered us kids
boxes of beads, long cigarettes dangling from their mouths.

You see? It turns out there are no islands
anyone can't get to, that we grow up

reading from some faraway place about the twenty-two
who tied themselves together with clothesline

in a downtown housing complex, the drunken hurricane
killing them anyway. Not like queens. Or even people.

Like bowling pins in an Alabaman Star Lanes.
There is the wasted but also the wasted.

Specificity, and yet I only want to kiss Martin's entire face.
Sobriety and anecdote are all that's keeping me

from saying so. He saw me the night of the storm,
stooped outside a local burrito barn, searching for my wallet

in a bush beside the parking lot, my free hand holding
an empty Corona bottle. There, only small clouds and small rains.

I assign too much homework, knowing the waves are good,
that Martin is looking out a window and into the coast,

hating me. The assignment has something to do with poems,
writing about a photograph from the New York Times,

a body lying dead on Prytania and surrounded by four orange traffic cones.
I want to say that now his red solo cup seems petrified and useless,

a reminder of something wasted and the approach of morning. We leave
the classroom silent, our binders pushing close to the chest.

Lou Dischler

Autobiography of an Innocent Man

1. I would have been born in swampland, but my father drove my mother to a city that day, a city with a stupid name, so I could forever be embarrassed by my birth certificate.

2. In the year of my birth, a shoe salesman was president. Well, perhaps he wasn't a shoe salesman, what did I know—I didn't wear shoes for another five years.

3. As a toddler, I was fed gumbo from an iron pot. The spices stunted my growth.

4. On weekends, my grandmother coated my teeth with flour and sticky sugars, and I became hyperkinetic.

5. My first love was fire. I watched her red hair, flickering so mysteriously, until I could not close my eyes, they were so dry.

6. One Sunday morning, all of the oxygen was breathed from the still air of the church, and I saw stars. A nun put smelly things under my nose, and I was embarrassed I'd called her ma'am.

7. Laika the dog flew around the earth and we heard her heart beating on the radio. My father was afraid. He said communists put that dog there, above our heads. He said I should study science, so we could put our own dog above our heads. I was confused—we had no dog.

8. My father was a teacher. I was six when he asked me to name the planets for his class. I was *the boy who could name the planets*, but I disappointed him—I forgot what came after Saturn. A giant girl took pity on me, and told a story on herself. She said she'd once believed we lived inside the earth, and that was why our rockets exploded. She was more than twice my age, but I knew she was an idiot.

9. In high school, I grew pubic hair. But it was a year too late.

10. After graduation, I moved to San Francisco, for the summer of love. But I missed it—another year too late.

11. In New Orleans I met a woman who wanted to be a writer but ended up a printer. And soon a judge in old Algiers said we were married.

12. Drinking tequila at a party, events were set in motion, and another judge said we were no longer married.

13. In ten short years I earned a bachelor's degree, with honors. I had listened to my father, and was ready to put a dog above his head.

14. Two summers later, my father was playing tennis, and then, on that same hot afternoon, he rolled on a highway until he was dead.

15. I stood up too suddenly at work and became dizzy. I confused that with love and became married for a second time.

16. The boy who cooks your hamburger in his burgundy and green uniform is more comfortable than other boys were ten years ago. He does not know it, but he owes his comfort to me.

17. One day my wife was driving down the interstate at seventy miles an hour when she insisted I open the door and step out. Soon a judge said we were no longer married.

18. For complicated reasons, an artist said words like troth, and I became married to my second wife's best friend.

19. At work, not so long ago, I stood up again too quickly and became dizzy. With insufficient oxygen, my mouth said things and I became unemployed.

20. In January, police came with cue tips and put my spit into an envelope. And, in the city where that shoe salesman had once lived, men in white coats I'd made comfortable years before said I was not a murderer.

Rick Mulkey

Summer, If It Ends At All, Ends Here

Sunset is lodged like a shard of glass
in the western sky. The day's heat
is pared down to something nearly benign.
Tomatoes on the vine swell deep red;
I pick one, juice spilling down my chin,
sweet acid on the tongue and throat.
Along the fence, rudbeckia towers over
the concrete bath where mocking birds
dip their heads and wings
then beat the air to smithereens.
The backyard is in a freefall.
The streetlamp releases its cone of light,
and what's veiled and unveiled enters me.
Coltrane, from the apartment next door,
blows *Giant Steps* so each breath suffers
to sound both wrong and right.
500 miles away, my mother's malignant
body sleeps after treatments,
hoping poison can kill poison.
Nothing beautiful about that healing,
the sores that open and swallow her up,
a remedy consumed with waste.
This is one kind of loneliness.
Another starts as muffled thunder
across the street before shouts and fists

spill out the screened door:
"I'll kill you, goddammit. I'll kill you."
The man's voice snaps at the woman
like a match to flame,
and the way the wind carries it,
a dry rasp over the scorched earth,
tells me he meant every word.

Toward Any Darkness

It returns, that dream of predatory flight,
soaring above dusk light, claiming little,
maybe the corn snake I'd thought lucky
shedding one body to live in another.
I rise, quiet, camouflaged, becoming one
of those middle-aged men
who watch from safe distances.
The great bird shreds the flesh,
drives its beak into the sinew
of something rank. The offal
ushered and unraveled
like Sunday morning's first hymn,
the notes beautiful and terrible all at once,
and the sweat on the preacher's brow
rising from some place unmentionable,
deep in the blind rookery of the body.
How do I keep the violence in?
Instinct moves me to smell the blood
and bone, hear the muscles' black
roots snapped from joints.
I fear nothing can weigh me down,
keep me from understanding
how this life I craft
could have been different,
could have been more

than bric-a-brac in a cupboard.
I step back from the window.
Wind rattles the outer walls.
In the fireplace flue, the wing-flutter
of startled wrens. Shadows,
roused from the boundaries,
stir toward any darkness.

Thermals

Sundays, when I was nine, we watched men disappear
into the sky, hang-gliders flying toward the Carolinas.
Less men than air, their buckles and loops chimed.
Even the steps they took, four quick steps before they threw
themselves over the cliffs, left no prints.
For a moment, my mother watched them
as they dropped below the edge,
when all we heard were trees scratching gliders.
She might have thought of my father rubbing her shoulders,
wings he called them, or she might have
looked across the valley and seen a glimpse
of the nights he'd disappear and how years later
by his bed, only she would stay with him through the night.
Or perhaps it was something as simple as the kites
we'd make later with brown paper and twine
and how no matter what we tried they never flew.
Watching my mother, I understood for the first time
the battles fought between gravity and flight.
For I saw her hold her breath as if it were
all she had left, as if by warming it beneath her breasts
she might release enough to give the gliders lift.
Each time one soared into view, my mother
breathed again. They flew all afternoon.

Autumnn in the Blue Ridge

Adrift in the garden's last Byzantine upswell:
no work, no obligation, no duty.
Only the percussion of the woodpecker
on the unyielding oak, the garish cardinal,
a single flame against hard frost,
the fattened squirrel filching acorns
from its neighbor. Occasionally,
the season's last worker bee, thin-winged
and laboring, rifles through the ripened holly,
berries mustering on fallen leaves. Without warning,
I begin to tap my feet, soaring in this thinning light
of possibility, the hunter moon hiding
behind its web of trees, the north wind a hymn
the world hums on its way to dying.

Field Theory

That first time, sun overhead,
the itch and chaff of burn on neck,
no wind or rain in sight, the season ill,
you decided to plow the field all day.
When we found your body slumped
beside the idling tractor,
the earth's thick slabs
splayed like your heart,
we didn't think you'd make it.
For twenty years you've lived,
we've lived, a kind of grief,
afraid of when, afraid of next.

Yesterday, I discovered my own heart's
been bad since birth—my blood
a thickened cream, all bubbling clot.
And now one eye gone dark, no shapes,
just shades of gray and black.
Walking this morning in wooded fields
much like our own, the lucid crack of frost,
the deep hued autumn oaks,
I think how the old poets had it right,
how eyes don't help us see.
It's those darker, hidden organs—

liver, lung, spleen—the old unfaithful heart.
And though I'm no oracular Tiresias
divining the lives of men,
I know the universe is full
of what's unseen: dark matter everywhere,
dark stars obscuring worlds,
strings of gravity dancing bluegrass sashays,
whole invisible galaxies of turn
and counter-turn we take on faith,
just like self and shadow-self, son and father,
the tandem heartbeats of binary stars.

Gail McCullough

Converse Heights, November First

I come out of the house, invisible in my sunglasses
and running shoes, up the street, toward the old school,
trotting along sidewalks bordered by pine straw
scorching in the heat, dodging a sheet of the Sunday
funnies. Underarms sticky, I turn toward shade and the quiet

of a small house with ivy pushing faces over a window.
I pass a yard with a headless dummy and snaggled
jack-o-lanterns that remember earnest children,
orange slime on their arms, carefully handling
a dull knife. At the corner a group sits on a porch,

a woman saying *they asked me if I was a witch*
and ha-ha-ha I told them I don't know.
Leaves pile against curbing like big brown
caterpillars. Under my feet, candy wrappers
dropped by children who lagged

behind their parents, surreptitiously sampling
unchecked treats. One pristine Tootsie Roll,
lost in the hurry, snugs against a tree root.
A porch hung with carefully tied ropes
creates a giant spider lair. I pass the house

where my widowed friend
and her new husband will live (back
yard perfect for cookouts and her dog)
acorns popping under my feet, spitting
ahead of me. A squirrel scolds. Four young boys

playing basketball against a house talk
in short bursts. *He could* they say *if only*
he would try. Over my head, a dead tree
hangs forked against its neighbor. Below,
water trickles through a cracked culvert

into an unmoving pool where
the retarded little black boy was found
drowned thirty years ago, our first summer.
Slower now, pulling up the hill, I stop
to speak to my neighbor tending her flowers.

They're crazy this year she says.

My Neighbor Solves His Leaf Problem

I want to forget I watched
what happened—white trucks
swaggering down the street wearing
thousands of dollars worth
of cranes and saws. Why
hadn't I honored

the grace and wisdom
of that old oak, the oracle
indwelling? Two weeks
went by while one by one
arms were amputated.
When the slavering saws

were let loose the snarl
burrowed through my brain
but worse was the void
at day's end after the trucks,
loaded, lumbered away, leaving
the oak and me to await their return.

The druid inside me wails
without words. I cannot speak
of how the sky is shocked,
                         bleeding blue.

Angela Kelly

Promise, Which is Next to Promiscuous in the Dictionary

You have promised people blueberry pancakes for breakfast
        (God, the drunken night!)
but there are no blueberries anywhere
        (out of season, my friend)
he goes out for them anyway
        (your mother says you don't deserve him)
you see the dedication in his shoulders,
but know failure will come in the cheap
box of blueberry Bisquick already in the cabinet.

Your guests, nevertheless, gobble up the blue artificial taste,
hungover enough to applaud your spatula,
to pour on Aunt Jemima syrup, to pluck up
bacon slices and sausage links and you just keep
the coffee flowing, strong and hot,
the Sunday Times circling the table, sports,
comics, the op-ed pages which fail to elicit
much conversation from the thick tongues.

Finally, sticky plates stacked in the sink, the griddle rinsed
and your guests are all upstairs, packing
for their departures, eating aspirin,
swilling Alka-Seltzer, stripping the sheets
        (who slept where?)

Even as he comes rushing back
        (a homing pigeon)
delivering two expensive pints of blueberries
        (tiny, not quite ripe)
and you have to sit down and eat them,
each bitter blue pearl a promise.

American Diaspora

The house of dreams came to rest on the bottom shelf,
in cardboard, an architectural panorama of all they wished for.
It featured an inviting front porch, intricate windows,
peaked gables of the attic—even a garden patio,
where roses would spill unchecked over the stone walls.
It was her story, a bastardized version of an English
cottage, they would plant in an American suburb.
She whispered it nightly to his sleeping neck
until he began to build it from left over boxes, thick glue.
He added the bay window overlooking the meadow.
Putting down the X-acto knife, his hand trembled.
It was the crown jewel.

Years passed in the walk-up apartment and they spoke less
and less of the garden of peppers, tomatoes, and zinnias.
The beagle pup lost his name, the roses their smell and color.
The diorama migrated from centerpiece of the kitchen table
to a corner in the bedroom, then the bottom shelf of the closet.
Now under sad shoes, the fake trees and mini-shrubs
have been tumbled gray with dust bunnies,
The front door found in the kitchen junk drawer,
alongside matchbooks, takeout menus, pens out of ink,
lids for empty jars that might be anywhere.

Our Brother

He was our brother
and sometimes there were frogs in our panty drawer,
pond water in our soda pop cans,
the lock on the diary might be sprung,
money missing from the piggy bank.

But he brought Tina a yellow kitten when she had the flu,
he beat up Mark Hughey for telling Sophie she was fat,
we could borrow any of his albums, but never EVER touch his stereo.
And when we proved inadequate at rolling one,
he gave us little pipes and a good red bong.

When he joined the Marines we stood in the street and bawled,
every letter he sent us have a joke in it and cartoons of fellow soldiers.
We did not watch the evening news and we hid when
our father began to screech about GD V-ET-NAMMMM.
Our mother grew thin and we tried to cook apple pies and come home
early.

He was our brother
and finally he came home with no ankle, an ivory cane.
But he wouldn't come to the Fourth of July picnic
and our father punched him in the face out in the garage.
He came to my wedding drunk with a black eye
and a Viet Cong ear to show the best man.

He married a Cindy, then a Linda, and a Nancy.
He was a maintenance man of interstate motels.
He loved trout fishing, the whine of Bob Dylan,
cheeseburgers, and PBR. He drove dirt track
stock cars with a custom made boot.
He came to the birthdays of our children
with magic acts and once, a pony.

Then one October, his best girlfriend, Marlena, left him,
her ex-huxband came to their apartment, smashed out the patio door,
dragged her off and she liked it. Our brother sat alone
in the apartment with rain pouring through the doors,
god knows the nationality or the year of that rain blowing in.
On his lap, little pawn shop gun that looked like a toy.

Aly Goodwin

Morning Walk with the Dog through a Cemetery in Spartanburg, SC, Where We Found Clovis McBain

It feels safe here among those
who'll do no more harm,
although they're time-consuming.
They whisper strange things like
the quieter you become,
the more you'll hear.
So I'm careful what I say.
Today we found Clovis McBain
almost obscured by dandelions
blooming semi-circle
around his headstone,
uprooted and resting on its side.
I thought to straighten it,
forgetting the weight of stone.
(Clovis says *Sh-h-h-h !*
Leave well enough alone.)
So I tell him about the man
whose house is in the Y
of the road, who wears a hat,
mulches the peach tree,
leans his tallness on a shovel,

watches me.

I can't always be there for you,
he said once but what I heard
was *I'll be there sometimes.*

October leaves from the water oak
gather in the cracks of Clovis McBain's
displaced marker as if to keep him warm
or teach him to let go
(as if he doesn't already know.)

The Poem I Never Wanted to Write

for Megan

Tonight I took her leash for a walk,
a sort of Megan pill to kill grief,
but there was this woman
who stopped me to say *Goodwin,*
my husband reads a goose bone
for the weather. As if I give a shit.
My dog just died, and I shot back,
well did you know a September
Spartanburg spider links
my front porch to the one next door?
She gaped so I advanced:
Just where does your husband do this?

In the constellation Orion.

Not used to walks on pavement,
I've hit the streets alone, a Pharos light
moving without direction in black night,
disinterested in which trees grow where,
blind to a possible Palladian Arch
crowning some forgotten doorway
that's seen better times,
tuned to little except cracks
in broken sidewalks.
The walking things off

worked better on the ground
in the mountains of home,
where minor suns were more plentiful
in days of frost, where Megan
chased brown bears through the valley
of the fallen giant chestnut trees,
cornered them in Flat Creek beyond,
and bit two lost hikers
just trying to find North.

Elizabeth Drewry

Locust Hill

Lizzie B. Davis is buried next to the road.
Driving past at 55, I turn my head in time to see
her stone name and wonder *What's the B for*.

She liked to know what was going on.
High on her father's shoulders, she tugged
his hair and kicked her small feet into his collar bones
to make him turn around and around.

Lizzie climbed a chestnut oak to spy
on the red-haired twins, deciding which one to marry;
chose the younger by three minutes for the way
he looked at her without dipping his head.

They built a flat-roofed house. No upstairs room to gaze from
but a porch she could sweep with an eye to the lane
and an eye to the field for her husband and sons—

the eldest freckled and big-boned like his father, and three more
dark and quick, stair-stepping into hand-me-downs. Her girl
was stillborn, the one time Lizzie turned her face to the wall.

It's dusk, and I switch on my headlights, catch the eyes
of a raccoon lumbering along the ditch.
The B stands for a name not bequeathed.

Walking tomorrow in that family plot, I'll trace a line
from stone to stone, touch the stark dates that shuttered
Lizzie from the long view she loved beyond and beyond.

Thanksgiving on Glassy Mountain

No one presides at this table. The mountain presides,
indisputable granite. Millennia of uplift and erosion
reduce our decades to a breath, a glimpse,
a nod. No wonder we tell stories
and inscribe epitaphs in igneous rock.

We are far from the thin air of boardrooms,
spectacle of careers like kiting hawks on thermals.
The dihedral glide, the plummet—and the mouse
scrabbling in brown leaves ascends, startled,
above wild turkeys fat-breasted and gleaning
for ripened seedheads in the binocular focus of the bobcat.

Along the winding road from Landrum we travel,
sacks filled with the makings of a feast. Sun-silvered snow
melts on manes of horses bent to fescue, and on peach trees,
low and squat, denuded but for brown-gray bark,
upper branches lighter, like flesh of inner arms upturned.
Shed of summer's heavy beauty, they revel
in plain dignity and proportion, a shape-note choir.

Behind our mountain chapel, tombstones erode over bones
of children—*Darling We Miss Thee* for Claud, four days alive,
Alice's son. And for Martha, daughter of Ola and John.
In neighboring blackgums, bees make honey, amber and peachy
with notes of caramel—the sweetness of life,
its undertone of longing deep and molten as magma.

Kris Neely

Spartanburg's Community Thanksgiving Service, 1996

Before I put on my tie
Momma coaxed me
into peeling two bags
of baking apples.

We hurried to leave them
towel-covered in sugared piles
within the waxy green bowls
to brown, waiting for night baking.

Grandma was coming for the feast.
The storm door smudged by five sizes
of hustling hands, and Momma honking
the car horn gently to say, "We are late again."

We wrestled for seats until we unloaded
the burnt umber convention van
on the asphalt of Central United Methodist,
an old church dwarfed by a 1950's office tower.

Walking through the heavy oak doors
into the buttercup stucco walls we scuffled
to the back pew, groaning to greet us,
during the minister's welcome.

The first hymn's beginning was startling.
A soft melody from behind the altar
sporadically suffocated with enormous blasts
of bass sounding from the hidden larger pipes.

I turned around and looked above to see
six towering silver cylinders on the back wall.
Worshipping the cosmic Atari, singing,
"We Gather Together," Mother shifted her position.

Laughter was forced into a compound—
half smirk, half offering envelope jottings.
She could not divide us into reverent pairings.
Father frowned from the podium seeing our unrest.

He delivered his prayer from the Psalms,
and slowly walked back to join us.
The parade of clerics continued to refrain
from acknowledging any definable creeds,

until the dark, deep-voiced preacher from
an urban black church stepped up against
the crackling microphone with a pop of power
and "Jesus" welled up from his four-button suit.

In a silent liturgical gasp the congregation cringed.
The Rabbi took it in stride and delivered us
a short sermon that filled his mouth with heavy h's.
I remember singing inside the techno-organ.

I recall feeling thankful for the blessings—
father's peppermints, given in exchange for silence,
the long awaited ending when the ties can come off,
and the apple crisp next to Grandma's brownies.

Emily Smith

Flat

*When the South does sorry,
there's nothing sorrier on earth.*
—Pat Conroy, *Beach Music*

When I was thirteen
all I wanted was every boy's lust.
That—and red panties.
I would sit at my mother's sewing
mirror and practice looks,
brush my hair until it was soft
and limp and then
needed washing again.
I would float in our pool
with my tortoise-shell sunglasses,
assemble suitors in my head
and then dry myself in the sun
like a painting or a sponge.

I was ready. I was worthy.
I hoarded books, bit my nails,
and after school I smoked
the stubs of my father's
Winston regulars
stolen from ashtrays
or sometimes the driveway
because I was just a regular kind of girl.
But I was smart—with a little red
in my hair and eyelashes as long as any boy's.
And I knew, grinding my singed filters

into the grass with my shoe, that someday
I would have one man's love,
that I'd be so pretty to him he'd want to cry.
And then all those other boys would be left
sitting cold, boots frozen in Woodruff,
and then wouldn't they be sorry.

Elvis

railroad tracks always cut like zippers at night
clipping silhouettes of ink-blot riders
to shove between the pages of a telephone book
or a bible
it's no different tonight
me, him, the smell of gasoline soaking in the floorboards

he likes my shirt,
likes it when the stripes go that way—
horizontal
I like it when he clips my thumb between two fingers,
his other hand finding me in the dark,
and then lets go

he holds everything like a cigarette.

the telephone rings in the hall
you should get that, he says,
voice crowded in his throat as he sits up
I forget about the darkness while I'm gone
and then he's beside me in a white wife-beater
shoulders cold porcelain,
hands on my hips

it's halloween somewhere outside
these dead-blue windows

he forgets, braces himself, forgets again
and then the sheets are unfolded, white and
cold through to the floor
that same cold porcelain—
that bathroom sink porcelain—
pinched between my knees

I can hear the train coming and listen,
surprised, too, at the noises I make.

everything is louder in the dark.

The House of My Mother is Falling Down

I.

When I was four, my father took my brother
and me to watch the city
implode an old hotel. It was winter
and I sat on his shoulders so I could see over the crowd,
the rust-colored building roped off and sinking in the mud.
When it happened, I don't remember the sound—
just the fall like melting,
the disappearing woman whose quiet empty clothes hit the
floor and my mother swatting at him to bring me down,
scared of sparks or falling dust or shards.

II.

My mother closes the bathroom door
to show me her new scar,
the same one I have, and we stand
with our shirts up in front of the mirror
talking about color and texture and direction—
the new glue they've sealed her with like mortar,
and she says *feel it*, the hard mass of scar
the size of a roll of quarters under her skin
and she says it doesn't hurt when my fingers graze it.

III.

It's an infection, my sister says. She knows it is
and I watch the two of them
huddled under the good kitchen light
inspecting the plum-colored stains on my mother's tongue.
I've seen them too and they look like the tiles
in our old shower, like bruises, mottled flesh
she swears she hasn't been biting in her sleep.
My sister takes her face in two sturdy hands and tilts it back,
says that Indian doctor doesn't know what she's doing,
asking about nightmares instead of looking at blood.

IV.

When my mother told me about the shingles
I imagined green ones like those torn off our roof
covering her back like armor, little pock marks
like a vest of protective scales, and when I'd scratch
her back for her, my feet sliding on the braided rug,
she said not to worry—I could never push too hard.

V.

Tonight I take clean laundry to her bedroom
and sit on the unmade bed, warm den of her sheets
and imagine her asleep, the fraying treacherous nerves,
bad wiring that could ignite her. A bottle of her Opium
is on the nightstand, and I remember how, as a child,
I thought the amber perfume looked edible—
a jar of Japanese honey, the hand crème
that came with it at Christmas, spiced coconut paste.
I worried then about it spoiling—about bees
and her melting in the rain, with that same sweet smell
I craved at night, watered down,
and only rising some mornings over the sheared wet lawn.

It's still melting and spoiling I worry about—
strong Denver foundation crumbling like damp
sugar, the body that made me funneling inward,
amber silt in the center of the crowd.

Elizabeth Cox

Teacher

What is imagined is real, you said.
The imaginer's eye makes me crazy sometimes.
It is blood caught in my pale heart, a river
going through the house. Blindness comes in,
like vision—perplexing the inner space.
Swans go on the surface, their wings lifting.
I would go with them anywhere.

That's good, you say. It's what I told
my daughter when she played our game: naming
something smaller than the other person named.
She was the smallest one herself, when she said,
"The black part of a baby ant's eye."
That's good, honey.
The one with the wildest dreams wins.

Try to remember the last time you
stepped into the bark of a tree,
closed it up behind you. A fat oak
with rings going around your arms like bells.
The sun can pull you taller in that deep
chamber of wood, and all your talk
becomes a wilderness.

When you step out from that,
you find the world is not what you thought.
Your earliest memory is not "of someone,"
but of green water, and cells changing, or skin.
You *are* as alone as you feared.
Think hard about the breath you take.
It is not like kissing.

I can do nothing, but shuffle these papers around
the desk, and put on my shoes. I am grateful
for the string in the hard dark that pulls me in,
for the imaginer, and for the pupil found
in the baby ant's eye—but mostly, for the flight
occurring in my daughter's young face,
when she spoke up, and won.

Under the Hickory Tree

for Ozella

The black face ate the persimmons whole,
a juice running slack and thin down her mouth.
The white child tasted the hickory
fallen from our oldest tree,
while stories dropped all day
from the black woman's soft, blunt face.
Her fingers could pull back the husks
to feed the child who wished to touch

her palms that smelled like wood,
or the half-moons of her fingernails.
Neither knew how to talk
of what was mounting under the tongue:
a hickory worked inside their words,
through years and days and nights
when the child would walk in sleep
to the room, to the lamp that burned all night,

and slip beneath the covers
where a drowsy black pulse
carried them toward morning.
And they spoke of what they wished for,
what could be found at the hickory nut tree
or in the taste of persimmons
that lay cold beneath the tongue,
like a coin lodged there forever.

Now you listen to me,
when they cut down that tree
you gonna count those rings,
you gonna see how they go out so far,
telling you how old they is,
and they so old it's like they was laughing,
like they was somebody down in there
that can't stop laughing.

When the crickets came at noon,
they rubbed their legs like saws
against a distant wood.
Ozella knew how trees were cut.
She taught me to eat persimmons whole,
to wear for Sunday around my neck
the clover chains we wove all day.
When she took me home she bathed me good.

The stumps grow flat and round today,
and rings of certain age start here,
where somebody deep inside the wood
throws back her head as if she could
never stop the laughing.
And the crickets have already come,
but they have not broken the chain we wove,
they have not taken the coin lodged under the tongue.

The Minister's Daughter

They tell me
the minister's daughter
is beautiful. Men call to her
from the road. She answers
back, pinned to her chair,
fluffing her hair in the light,
her dress undone at the waist.
She will not walk in her sleep,
or in her own lifetime.

She stares down the long valley,
and admits to herself, she wants
to do the most outrageous thing.
In the number of years she has left,
to lift one heavy foot and put it
like a fist into the ground.
She wants to stop the old couples
from coming to the house, stop
them from bringing loaves,

handing them like small
birds about to be crushed.
When she goes in to dinner,
her body is carried, her legs
hang over her father's arm,

not like a lover,
not with the promise of something to come,
but proper, like an ant
carrying another ant's head.

(If)

If the horizon in the west bruised by the coming night could grow legs
and walk toward the world, if it could walk toward
the people and houses of our life,

Or if the line of a far place could approach us with beautiful feet, would we listen?

If the top of a tall pine, loaded with green spring cones, bent down
to put the cone beside our ear, would we believe what was whispered?
The cone having a perspective of height.

If a stranger comes to the door, do we get a gun?

If someone loves us, do we feel obligated?

Where does joy go, when we don't feel joyful? Where does the orange tongue
of anger split and linger?

If the birds on their tiny legs in the dust choose not to fly, do we judge them?

Why do we turn sons into soldiers? Why do we put together millions
of young men, troops taught to startle and murder?

If we are not violent, are we then good? Do we pretend
to be good, while waiting for violence to come back in again?

Why do we make business and everyday work a war? Why do we teach
the young that winning is everything?

Who is in charge of careful attentiveness?

If we are backed against the wall, do we tell the truth at that time?

If the brook water pulls itself deliberately over the rocks and flows to the place of river or sea, do we follow or just watch?

If we know the presence of sunlight even when the ground and sky are gray, then why do we despair?

Say This

Say that a river flooded the house.
Say water rose up to ruin all that was owned.
Say that the water covered the whole town for a time,
sweeping toys and hats, photos, skillets,

hammers into a place downriver.
Then, without warning, the water recedes
and that town is left exposed to the wind.
Same town—soaked, recognizable.

People become daily forms bending down
to search for pieces of what they had owned,
bowls floating in a tree. How terrible the damage:
snakes in kitchen cabinets or turtles on a chair,

cows floating toward some bridge, caught, strangled.
After this day, everyone knows something old about life,
one intimate, or devastating, fact.
So what is important now?

All that came before this day is mocked;
but behind the eyes of the town
a new image forms, a thousand fragments rise
up from the flood into one whole piece.

What is dreaming, after all—
but the ebb and flow of something that comes
to wash away all we have, so that we can
make way for any unthought-of possibility.

The task, then, is to define that new piece,
to know its weight and structure, its edge
above the water, the new shoreline
that wobbles according to the water's lapping.

Jennie Neighbors

Morning Song

Gives rise, this rising and this falling, a rising and darker world. A morning song so fledged it can include the long shadows of itself.

You stand where you are, the only unendurable instant, losing the thread.

—a song for us, so fledged

Thought

        outside edge
of the inside

fits
        and starts

Landscapes are a preparation for what will later appear as a set. A certain number a story always slips into, or tends to.

The Direction the Poem Must Travel

                    rising and falling with the horizon
chances are the found object
that you:
                    altering, destroying, etc.

the border, its shimmering edge

standing on, looking

Robert Mullins *aka Moody Black*

Still Home

Sparkle City, this itty-bitty mini-metropolis
Otherwise, known as home
I feel alone
But I love the cuisine, fish and grits and greens
Macaroni and cheese, whole corn or cream
We're born to dream, finer things and such
But livin' in Sparkle City makes it hard to touch
No matter what, it's still home—it's hard to fuss
The "Bible-Belt" got us lookin' for a god to trust
It ain't much, but the renaissance tryin' to rise
They got plans, tryin' to expand the skyline
Where the sunset rests on downtown's chest
Where mill villages and projects plagued with stress
Some say they're blessed just to deal with the mess
Cause home is where the heart is to feel through the flesh
You got to filter through tests, and Sparkle City is that
Just one big test
So, take one big breath
And exhale home: bitter-sweet it is
It's so simple, but deep
Like *The Secret* is
Cause my people live one day at a time
The southern breeze and southern trees plant seeds in the mind
I love/hate "The Burg" 'cause we go through things
In this show called life, we go through scenes

Like racial undertones, and *Attack of the Clones*
Misled juveniles who claim to be grown
And just to *Do the Right Thing* seems too complex
When the people from Falcon Crest criticize the projects
And the project people become numbers for stats
While some settle for the stereotype for the act
In fact, "it's like a jungle, sometimes it makes me wonder ..."
And that's just it ... it only makes me wonder
So, I capture the footage: "action" and "cut"
It seems we're only superstars at the first of the month
And tryin' to find a place to fit is like findin' a place to sit
I've tried to escape, but I'm back in the mist
It's worldwide, I seen it before—it's well known
Cause no matter what goes on, you still go home

Butler Brewton

Walnut Grove Plantation

On visiting an old plantation in Spartanburg County

Still, Walnut Grove Plantation
Peeks out of tall dark trees
Standing like silent sentries
Against a changing world;

I dare to walk these flat white stones
Quietly leading to an old door sealed;
But there's no master of this house,
Nor wife, nor daughters sewing here
In the haven of some upper room;
And, no sons attend the father's school,
Though quills and rulers rest in peace—
Remnants preserved in dust that settled
In centuries of passing time.

But I hear a bustling of busy feet
Around a kitchen's flaming hearth;
And footfalls sound through empty halls
While glasses tinkle in the Keeping Room;
Some night-caller hails outside
Where dirt path is lit by the moon;

And it seems I see my father's fingers
Or his father's father's hands
Scribbling some indecipherable appeal

Over this wide and woody land;
And I see dark women standing,
Though they kneel at the spinning wheels.
I can't tell you if I dream,
Or if this journey here is real,
But I think I smell gunpowder
And hear a church bell peal;

And there's this mournful singing
Far beyond the tinkling glasses;
There's a weeping people bending
Cutting cane stalks for molasses;
There're wagons on the hillside
Filled with hay for grazing cattle;
There're strong young men logging
Yet I hear their shackles rattle.

Lord, then, how do I tell the children
There's something else I find
Out here in this Walnut Grove
Buried deep within the mind—
Something fossilized with the order
And the anguish of its time,
And I have no words nor whim
That will capture it for them.

But you can see it in the meadow
When the sparrow lifts its wings;
You can hear it in the music
When you hear the southland sing;
Mostly, you will feel it in the clutches
Of the Spartanburg embrace,
And it's as sweet as honeysuckle

Or the shy girl's tender lips;
Something's rooted in the backbone,
Feels like love that never ends;
It's some deepened soul relation
That binds southerners as friends.
Oh, you people who are kissed
By the scorching sun's bright sky,
I can tell you about our kindred
For I've seen us eye-to-eye:

We are the truest spirit
In the core of America's soul;
And together we've birthed a nation
From the Walnut Grove Plantation.
Men of oceans, women of seas,
Blood of a culture eternally,
Listen to the hoot-owl's hooting
And the whippoorwill's brave song;
And the children's tender fingers
That have not yet sketched the notes
Will unearth and play our harmony
From the crevices of history.

So, Walnut Grove, rest easy
Deep in your order and misery,
Your southern yang and yin;
There is no argument in me,
Thankful that I am here to see
Where my roots were made so sturdy,
And what has made me sing!
Keep the rivers and the valleys,
The green vines and the walnut trees;
And let the old home's spirit rally,

Salute the history in me.
Take my hand, my mighty people;
I will lead you on these stones
Of our archetypal essence:
Marrow in ancestral bones.
Nothing's like the troubled past,
And the laughter in the Keeping Room
When the two united at last
In dignity and proud honor
Of the South, our common womb.

Peach Orchard

Still I hear the flatbed truck
Rumbling down the road before sunup,
Waking me to the chatter of strong—
Shouldered men with loose shirts
Smelling of Borax,
The high-pitched voices of girls
Waiting, crowding together for the pickup.

Mama will call us soon to get about
The yard work when it's light enough
To hitch out the cow in the high dewy
Grass that stings the ankle sores
That never heal all summer.

The chickens are to be fed,
The hog slopped with the leftovers;
The old dog covered with ticks
Will wag his tail expecting a handout;
The kittens will cower underneath the barn.

And when the sun's too hot,
We young ones will play under the wild
Cherry tree, getting drunk on the berries,
Press our feet into the dry dirt
Until the sun moves beyond us,
And the shade disappears into evening.

It'll be time to gather things in,
Latching up for night—
The time for washing feet,
To listen for the old truck coughing
Out of the distance on quiet wheels,
Bringing folks back from the orchards,
Ashy folks, their faces
Stinging from peach fuzz.

To a Lady of the South

I think the water
Must be good,
Or your food is cut fresh
From the garden;
Maybe it's the golden sun
Over the kudzu
That has been so kind to you;

Whatever it is,
It has made you firm
In body and mind,
Beautiful and strong enough
To be this kind,

And at the same time
As soft as goose feathers
And as sweet as nectar
In magnolia blooms.

Late afternoons
I see you sitting beneath umbrellas,
Your skin as mellow as melon,
You are sipping sweet tea,
Silently wise enough to know,
With your big southern eyes,
How you are getting to me.

Grandpa's Oak

I counted 217 circles
In the oak stump when we cut it down
To clear the east sky,
Letting the morning sunlight
Into the back lot behind the house;
I smelled the raw wood for days,
Chewing on strips to taste the sap,
Sticky and sweet, fresh
Like the juice in cane stalks;

We burned the last of the logs
Last winter during Grandpa's wake,
But the stump is still there,
Where the tree was felled,
With toadstools blooming up
Around the roots, mushrooms
Blighting the old bark
Like some skin disease
With the pimples ripe;

Nothing's left in the sky
Were black birds used to fly
To their nests built on the limbs
That once filled the space
Like the big arms of a giant
Held high, proud and ageless,

Just a few wispy early clouds
Floating like puffs of smoke
From an old man's pipe.

Rafters

The barn,
Gray and rotten
Near where the edges
Touch the wet earth,
Is filled to the rafters
With things we put away
From one year to the next;

And out in the field,
Half hidden by the wild sprouts,
Is the old plow my father left
The last year he planted the crop
We all deserted,
Never harvesting what his sweat
Was meant for,

But left one by one
Taking wives and husbands
In the cities where the work
Was good in the factories.

We sat on the hot cement stoops
Drinking beer on paydays
While our children grew
Farther from our reach,

And one day
So far they could not hear
The sound of our voices
Calling through the night.

I know now that what we came for
We didn't get, and we have put away
Whatever plans we had.
I will go back
And try to pull the old plow
Out of the land,
Fix the bottom of the barn
With aging hands.

Contributors

PHILIP BELCHER has published poems in a variety of poetry journals including *Plainsong*, *Thorny Locust*, and *Free Lunch*. In 2005, he won the Porter Fleming Writing Competition Prize in Poetry and he was also selected as the 2006 South Carolina Poetry Fellow Alternate by the South Carolina Arts Commission. In 2007, Philip's chapbook, *The Flies and Their Lovely Names*, was published by Stepping Stone Press. He is a member of the Academy of American Poets and for several years has been a member of SPOETS, a Spartanburg-based poetry group. Philip's parents were born and reared in Inman, South Carolina, in northern Spartanburg County. His maternal grandmother graduated from one of the first nursing classes at what was then known as Spartanburg General Hospital and his maternal grandfather was a pharmacist in Inman. Philip's paternal grandparents owned and operated a peach farm along what is now Belcher Road in northern Spartanburg County. Since 2000, Philip has served as President of the Mary Black Foundation, a health foundation serving Spartanburg County. Philip is a graduate of Furman University, Southeastern Baptist Theological Seminary, and the Duke University School of Law.

BUTLER E. BREWTON, a native of Spartanburg, is a Professor Emeritus from Montclair State University in New Jersey where he taught English for twenty-five years. After retirement he began teaching poetry at Furman University in Greenville, South Carolina. He holds a BA in English, an MA in English, and a PhD in English from Rutgers University. His poetry has appeared in many publications, "Rafters" winning First Prize in *Essence*. He has published three collections of poetry and has had two essays published by the Hub City Writers Project. Although poetry is Dr. Brewton's great passion, he has published articles, critical essays, short fiction, and edited a sixteen-volume encyclopedia while in London. He presently lives with his wife, Blanca, in Simpsonville, South Carolina.

ELIZABETH COX has published poems in *Kentucky Review*, *The Southern Review*, *The Atlantic Monthly*, and others, and her short stories have been cited for excellence in both Best American Short Stories and Pushcart Press. One story, *Third of July*, was chosen for the O. Henry Award Collection. A book of stories, *Bargains in the Real World*, was published by Random House in 2002. Ms. Cox has published four novels, including *Familiar Ground*, *The Ragged Way People Fall out of Love*, and *Night Talk,* which won the Lillian Smith Award. This award chooses books that raise the social consciousness and promote harmony between the races. Her newest novel, *The Slow Moon*, was published by Random House in 2006. Cox taught creative writing at Duke University for seventeen years. She held the Jack Kerouac Writer-in-Residence at UMass-Lowell and taught at MIT in the Program in Writing and Humanistic Studies. She also teaches in the Bennington Writing Seminars and presently shares the John Cobb Chair of Humanities at Wofford College with her husband, C. Michael Curtis.

LOU DISCHLER grew up in Louisiana where he often waded through waist-deep floods, avoiding the fire ants that piled up by the millions to form rafts. If you touched one, they'd climb all over you, thinking you were dry land. Once he ran around in the eye of a hurricane—he must've been six at the time. When he moved to Spartanburg another hurricane followed him, but he managed to bottle it and make it do his bidding. He was an engineer by then, so doing that was easy. When he began writing novels, he did away with the weather altogether. He wrote thrillers where he drowned, stabbed, and mutilated the characters in the most horrible fashion, yet the sun shined down on them pleasantly, and there was never a hurricane to deal with. He is a first-place winner in the annual Hub City Prize for poetry.

ELIZABETH DREWRY wrote and edited poetry for small-press journals before her writing career was interrupted by twenty years in the newspaper business. Now retired with her husband to the foothills of the Blue Ridge Mountains, she has resumed her first passion. Elizabeth was delighted to discover the thriving writers' communities of South Carolina, including Spartanburg's own Hub City Writers Project.

EDWIN C. EPPS is a National Board Certified teacher at Spartanburg High School. He is the author of *Literary South Carolina* (Hub City Writers Project, 2004) and the former editor of *South Carolina Writing Teacher*. His poetry has appeared in *POINT*, *The Savannah Literary Journal*, *Drift*, and the anthologies *Out of Unknown Hands*, *Rhythms*, *Reflections and Lines on the Back of a Menu*, *The Southern Poetry*

Anthology Volume I: South Carolina and elsewhere. He is currently at work on a book to be called *Beautiful Duncan Park: A Father and Son Explore a Classic American Ballpark.*

MARCEL GAUTHIER has been the Upper School Director and an English instructor at the Spartanburg Day School for the past five years. Before he moved to Spartanburg with his family, he taught for eight years at The Potomac School (right across the street from the CIA!) in McLean, Virginia, and for four years at the Brentwood School in Los Angeles, California. A graduate of Dartmouth College, Marcel completed his MFA in Poetry at the University of North Carolina-Greensboro, where he was a Randall Jarrell Fellow. The recipient of a grant from the National Endowment for the Humanities, he has most recently published poetry in *The Old Red Kimono, Timber Creek Review, Spoon River Review, Tampa Review,* and *The South Carolina Literary Review.* He has a poem forthcoming in *The Southeast Review.*

ALY GOODWIN, native of North Carolina, was educated at UNC-Asheville, Converse College, Erskine College, and the University of Iowa Writer's Workshop. Her work has appeared in several publications, including *Southern Poetry, Vol. 1: South Carolina, A Millennial Sampler of South Carolina Poetry, BayLeaf, The Iowa Review, Appalachian Review,* and the *News & Observer.* She is a recipient of the Marjorie Peale Award from the Poetry Society of South Carolina, and she is a charter member of SPOETS, a Spartanburg-based group of poets.

FRANCES L. HARDY is a lifelong resident of Spartanburg. She holds degrees from Wofford College, Converse College, and the University of South Carolina. Hardy has been published in anthologies and educational journals. She has also published two books of poetry—*Risings* and *Peace Weaving.* Hardy has received grants from the Spartanburg Arts Partnership to promote her poetry and the works of local writers. She teaches language arts at Spartanburg High School, and she is a 2007–2008 Honor Roll Teacher for the State of South Carolina.

THOMAS L. JOHNSON, retired Librarian Emeritus from the University of South Carolina, has won numerous awards for his work as a poet, short fiction writer, and editor, most notably the Lillian Smith Award for his 1986 book, *A True Likeness.* The "Note on a Nightscape" here was produced out of the 2006 poetry tutorial conducted by Anita Skeen at Converse College. The "Nine Haiku" suite is honorific verse written upon the departure from Spartanburg of a fellow member of SPOETS, the writing group he co-founded in 2003.

ANGELA KELLY was awarded a Poetry Fellowship from the South Carolina Arts Commission in 1999. She is the author of four poetry chapbooks, most recently *Post Script from the House of Dreams* (winner of the 2006 South Carolina Poetry Initiative Prize, Stepping Stone Press.) In 2008 Backwater Press is publishing her full-length volume of poetry, entitled *Voodoo for the Other Woman.* She has had individual poems published in numerous journals, including *North American Review*, *The Bloomsbury Review*, *Nimrod*, *The Asheville Poetry Review*, *Kalliope*, *Rhino*, *Yemassee*, *Inkwell*, *Rosebud*, *The Ledge*, and *Rattle*. She has been awarded fellowships from the Virginia Center for the Creative Arts and the Vermont Studio Center.

JOHN LANE grew up in Spartanburg, his mother's ancestral home. A Wofford alumnus with an MFA in poetry from Bennington College, Lane was the recipient of the Henry Hoyns Fellowship at the University of Virginia, an NEA Apprenticeship grant at Copper Canyon Press, and the South Carolina Fellowship in Poetry in 1984. He has taught creative writing, literature, and film at Wofford since 1988. Lane is also the editor of Holocene Publishing and co-founder of the Hub City Writers Project. In 1995 his book of poems, *Against Information & Other Poems*, was widely reviewed and prompted appearances on Canadian and National Public Radios and a front-page review in *Small Press Review*. In 2000 he was awarded the Phillip H. Reed Memorial Award for Writing on the Southern Environment from the Southern Environmental Law Center. Lane is the editor, with Gerald Thurmond, of *The Woods Stretched for Miles: New Southern Nature Writing* from the University of Georgia Press, which also published his three books of creative nonfiction, *Waist Deep in Black Water* (2002), *Chattooga: Descending into the Myth of Deliverance River* (2004), and *Circling Home* (2007).

GAIL MCCULLOUGH received an MLA from Converse College in 2002 and an MFA from Queens University of Charlotte in 2005. Her BA came from Wake Forest College in 1958. She turned to writing and reading poetry after years of reading anything but poetry. A chronic bookaholic, Gail presented her Queens craft seminar on the books she had purchased during her studies there—numbering over forty, in addition to the syllabi. She has lived in Spartanburg in the same house for almost forty years. She is engaged in a dirty battle with her neighbors for yard honors.

MAMIE MORGAN was raised in Spartanburg and attended Wofford College where she studied English and Religion. She completed her MFA at UNC-Wilmington and now serves as the poet-in-residence at the South Carolina Governor's School of Arts and Humanities. She grew up defending her way through the alleyways of

Converse Heights, hiding under her father's desk at Converse College, wading in galoshes along Lawson's Fork, and tending bar at various local establishments. Her work is forthcoming in *The Greensboro Review*.

RICK MULKEY is the author of four poetry books: *Toward Any Darkness*, *Bluefield Breakdown*, *Greatest Hits 1994-2004*, and *Before the Age of Reason*. Individual poems and essays have appeared in such journals as *Shenandoah*, *Poetry East*, *Denver Quarterly*, *Southern Poetry Review*, *The Literary Review*, *Connecticut Review*, *Poet Lore*, *Crab Orchard Review*, and in several anthologies including *American Poetry: The Next Generation* and *A Millennial Sampler of South Carolina Poetry*. Among his awards are the Charles Angoff Award from *The Literary Review* and a Hawthornden Fellowship for a writing residency in Edinburgh, Scotland. Mulkey has taught creative writing and American literature at colleges, universities, and writing workshops in the United States and Europe. Most recently, he directed the MFA Creative Writing program at Wichita State University. He currently teaches poetry and American literature at Converse College, where he directs the creative writing major.

ROBERT MULLINS, a.k.a. Moody Black, is a Spartanburg native who electrifies audiences across the country with his original poems and energetic performances. Fusing a blend of hip-hop, soul, and poetry, he delivers a unique rhythmic message in which each new listener finds common ground. Moody Black has been a performing artist since the age of twelve and has become a prominent force on a multi-regional poetry scene through his enthusiastic live shows and strong work ethic. He performs at public schools and colleges and hosts the monthly poetry night at the T.K. Gregg Recreation Center. He was featured on a Turner South "My South" commercial shot in 2005. Moody served as Poetry Slam Master (Captain) for the 2006 and 2007 Upstate Slam Poetry Team.

KRISTOFER M. NEELY serves as Director of the Success Initiative at Wofford College. The fourth son of Dr. and Mrs. Kirk H. Neely, Kris developed his interdisciplinary approach to art in the back pews of churches throughout the city of Spartanburg. A creative writer and a visual artist, Kris served as writer-in-residence and editor for *Hidden Voices: Reflections from an Affected Community*, a community-based art project published by the Hub City Writers Project and sponsored by the Arts Partnership of Greater Spartanburg and Piedmont Care, Inc. in 2005. Kris's visual work was featured in *This Threshold: Writing on the End of Life*, published in 2007 by Hub City. Kris and his wife, Patrice, make Spartanburg their home.

SCOTT NEELY grew up in Spartanburg. He is the author of *A Good Road to Walk* (Holocene, 2000) and editor of *This Threshold: Writing on the End of Life* (Hub City Writers Project, 2007). Scott serves as the Director of Mission at Spartanburg's First Presbyterian Church.

JENNIE NEIGHBORS' first book, *Between the Twilight and the Sky*, will be published in Fall 2008 by Parlor Press. Her work has appeared in Ugly Duckling Presse's Poste Card Series, *Osiris*, *neotrope*, *Dirigible*, *gestalten*, and elsewhere. She received her MFA from Naropa University's Jack Kerouac School of Disembodied Poetics, and she is a Wisconsin Arts Board Fellow. She has lived in Spartanburg since 2003 with her husband, Jim, and her son, Esten. She loves her new friends and her Wofford students.

FRED PARRISH was born in Greenville, South Carolina and graduated from Wofford College with a BA in English in 1963. He worked at Spartan Mills for thirty-six years and, since 2002, has been writing nature notes and speeches, clearing trails, building boardwalks and bridges, and taking inventory of flora and fauna for SPACE, the Spartanburg Area Conservancy. Fred and his wife, Patrice, have four children: Frederick, Melissa, Jenny, and Susanna.

ALEX RICHARDSON has one collection of poetry, *Porch Night on Walnut Street* (Plain View Press, 2007), and he teaches creative writing at Limestone College, where he is chair of the English department. He studied poetry at the University of South Carolina and at the Center for Writers at University of Southern Mississippi. He grew up in Greenville with dreams of making it out, and so far he's made it as far as Spartanburg. He has lived in east Spartanburg for eight years, and he recognizes everyone he sees whenever he leaves home.

EMILY SMITH is a native of Woodruff, a small town in southern Spartanburg County. She attended Wofford College, where, in addition to studying biology, she also rediscovered her love of writing—a love that had been lost for two years in the tumultuous transition from high school to college. With the help of a devoted faculty, she graduated in 2006 and also received the 2005 Benjamin Wofford Prize for poetry, allowing the publication of *Baboon Heart*, a collection of poems. After a foray into bio-diesel in central North Carolina, Emily now resides serendipitously in the Florida Panhandle. From the outskirts of Sopchoppy, a town even smaller than Woodruff and where bears roam the dirt roads, she tends her small garden and often thinks fondly of home.

Born in Woodruff, **P. L. THOMAS** attended public schools in lower Spartanburg County before attending college at Spartanburg Methodist and USC-Spartanburg for his undergraduate work and the University of South Carolina for his doctorate. A life-long resident of Spartanburg County, Thomas has also published widely, primarily scholarly work related to teaching, writing, and literature. He currently is an assistant professor of education at Furman University where he often supervises pre-service and early career teachers in both Greenville and Spartanburg counties. He writes in and edits a series for Peter Lang USA with his next volume to be published in 2008, *Reading, Learning, Teaching Ralph Ellison*.

DENO TRAKAS writes poetry, fiction, essays, and e-mails in his office at Wofford College, where he is a professor of English. The Trakas family has lived in Spartanburg since 1900 when Nicholas Trakas settled here, the first Greek to do so. Deno is one of Nicholas's thirty-one grandchildren, and he is writing a book for Hub City about the Greeks of this area. He has two chapbooks, *The Shuffle of Wings* and *human and puny*, both published by Holocene Press. Three of his short stories are featured in Hub City's award-winning fiction collection, *New Southern Harmonies: Four Emerging Fiction Writers*.

Acknowledgements

The Hub City Writers Project gratefully acknowledges permission from the following contributors and their publishers to reprint poems in this volume.

Philip Belcher: "A Man Over Forty Discovers His Right Brain and Falls in Love with Her," "Estate Planning," "Mid-Life," "Natural History," and "Variations on the Word 'Chain'" from *The Flies and Their Lovely Names*, Stepping Stone Press, 2007. "Estate Planning" originally appeared in *Mobius* (Vol. 19, No. 2, 2004).

Butler Brewton: "To a Lady of the South" and "Walnut Grove Plantation" from *Indian Summer*, Sunbelt Books, 1997; "Grandpa's Oak" appeared in *Essence*; "Peach Orchard" appeared in *Nimrod*; "Rafters" from *Rafters*, Sunbelt Books, 1995.

Elizabeth Cox: "The Minister's Daughter," from *Homewords, A Book of Tennessee Writers*, Tennessee Arts Commission and The University of Tennessee Press, 1986; "Under the Hickory Nut Tree" appeared in *Green River Review, Anthology of North Carolina Poets*, Spring, 1983; "Say This," appeared in *The Southern Review*, Winter, 2007.

Edwin C. Epps: "After Reading James Still" has been published twice. First in Vol. 4, No. 51 of *Point* (Jan. 1994), then in *Savannah Literary Journal* (1997).

Frances Hardy: "Storage" from *Peace Weaving*, self-published.

Angela Kelly: "American Diaspora," "Our Brother," and "Promise, Which is Next to Promiscuous in the Dictionary," from *Post Script from the House of Dreams*, Stepping Stone Press, 2007.

John Lane: "Bethesda Road" from *As The World Around Us Sleeps*, Briarpatch Press, 1992; "Sweet Tea" and "Nostalgia for Work and Deep Mountains" from *Against Information & Other Poems*, New Native Press, 1995; "My Dead Father

Visits My Mother" and "My Dead Father Watches Traffic Pass" from *The Dead Father Poems,* Horse & Buggy Press, 2000.

Mamie Morgan: "Fall Term, 2005" appeared in *The Greensboro Review.*

Rick Mulkey: "Autumn in the Blue Ridge," "Field Theory," "Summer, If It Ends At All, Ends Here," "Thermals," and "Toward Any Darkness" from *Toward Any Darkness*, Word Press, 2007; "Autumn in the Blue Ridge" appeared in *Connecticut Review*; "Field Theory" previously appeared in *Talking River Review*; "Summer, If It Ends At All, Ends Here," also appeared in *Poet Lore*; "Thermals" previously appeared in *Southern Poetry Review*; "Toward Any Darkness" appeared in *Shenandoah.*

Jennie Neighbors: "Morning Song," "The Direction the Poem Must Travel," and "Thought" from *Between the Twilight and the Sky*, Parlor Press Free Verse Editions, 2008.

Alex Richardson: "Dancing Suite," "Digging up Azaleas Easter Eve," "Paradise Off Main," and "The Geometry of Commitment" from *Porch Night on Walnut Street*, Plain View Press, 2007; "Dancing Suite" appeared in *New Rag Rising*; "Paradise Off Main" appeared in *Poetry Motel*; "The Geometry of Commitment" appeared in *Main Channel Voices.*

Emily Smith: "Elvis," "Flat," and "The House of My Mother is Falling Down" from *Baboon Heart*, Holocene Press, 2006.

Deno Trakas: "After Reading Your Dead Father Poems," "Defining Family," "Labor Day, Pen and Spade," and "The Smaller House," from *human & puny*, Holocene Press, 2001; "Labor Day" appeared in *In the West of Ireland*, Enright House, 1992; "After Reading Your Dead Father Poems" and "The Smaller House" appeared in *A Millennial Sampler of South Carolina Poetry*, Ninety-Six Press, 2005 and *The Southern Poetry Anthology*, Texas Review Press, 2007.

The Hub City Writers Project is a non-profit organization whose mission is to foster a sense of community through the literary arts. We do this by publishing books from and about our community; encouraging, mentoring, and advancing the careers of local writers; and seeking to make Spartanburg a center for the literary arts.

Our metaphor of organization purposefully looks backward to the nineteenth century when Spartanburg was known as the "hub city," a place where railroads converged and departed. At the beginning of the twenty-first century, Spartanburg has become a literary hub of South Carolina with an active and nationally celebrated core group of poets, fiction writers, and essayists. We celebrate these writers—and the ones not yet discovered—as one of our community's greatest assets. William R. Ferris, former director of the Center for Southern Studies, says of the emerging South, "Our culture is our greatest resource. We can shape an economic base...And it won't be an investment that will disappear."

Hub City Anthology • John Lane & Betsy Wakefield Teter, editors

Hub City Music Makers • Peter Cooper

Hub City Christmas • John Lane & Betsy Wakefield Teter, editors

New Southern Harmonies • Rosa Shand, Scott Gould, Deno Trakas, George Singleton

The Best of Radio Free Bubba • Meg Barnhouse, Pate Jobe, Kim Taylor, Gary Phillips

Family Trees: The Peach Culture of the Piedmont • Mike Corbin

Seeing Spartanburg: A History in Images • Philip Racine

The Seasons of Harold Hatcher • Mike Hembree

The Lawson's Fork: Headwaters to Confluence • David Taylor, Gary Henderson

Hub City Anthology 2 • Betsy Wakefield Teter, editor

Inheritance • Janette Turner Hospital, editor

In Morgan's Shadow • A Hub City Murder Mystery

Eureka Mill • Ron Rash

The Place I Live • The Children of Spartanburg County

Textile Town • The Hub City Writers Project

Come to the Cow Pens! • Christine Swager

Noticing Eden • Majory Heath Wentworth

Noble Trees of the South Carolina Upstate • Mark Dennis, John Lane, Mark Olencki

Literary South Carolina • Edwin Epps

Magical Places • Marion Peter Holt

When the Soldiers Came to Town • Susan Turpin, Carolyn Creal, Ron Crawley, James Crocker

Twenty: South Carolina Poetry Fellows • Kwame Dawes, editor

The Return of Radio Free Bubba • Meg Barnhouse, Pate Jobe, Kim Taylor

Hidden Voices • Kristofer Neely, editor

Wofford: Shining with Untarnished Honor, 1854-2004 • Doyle Boggs, JoAnn Mitchell Brasington, Phillip Stone

South of Main • Beatrice Hill, Brenda Lee, compilers

Cottonwood Trail • Thomas Webster, G.R. Davis, Jr., Peter L. Schmunk

Comfort & Joy: Nine Stories for Christmas • Kirk Neely, June Neely Kern

Courageous Kate: A Daughter of the American Revolution • Sheila Ingle

Common Ties • Katherine Davis Cann

Spartanburg Revisited • Carroll Foster, Mark Olencki, Emily L. Smith

This Threshold: Writing on the End of Life • Scott Neely